How Birds Fly

Steve Cushman

ISBN-13: 978-0999787304
ISBN-10: 0999787306

UNIVERSITY
P R E S S

St. Andrews University Press

St. Andrews University
(A branch of Webber International University)
1700 Dogwood Mile
Laurinburg, NC 28352
press@sa.edu
(910) 277-5310

Also by Steve Cushman

Portisville (2004, Novello Literary Award winning novel)

Fracture City (2008, Short Stories)

Heart with Joy (2010, Novel)

Hospital Work (2013, Poetry Chapbook)

Midnight Stroll (2016, Poetry Chapbook)

Hopscotch (2017, Novel)

For Trevor

Specials thanks to Mike Gaspeny, Gwen Hart, and Dan Albergotti for reading many of these poems and offering valuable insight along the way.

Contents

1

2

3

1

How Do Birds Fly?

my son asks tonight before bed.
He's five and I'm trying to read

The Magic School Bus to him, but he's having
none of this story, because earlier

at the park he came to me,
pulled me by the hand

and showed me a dead sparrow
beneath the slide.

When I said we should leave it alone,
he said no we had to do something

and of course he was right
so we did what I didn't want to do

brought the bird home
buried it in the backyard

tied together two popsicle sticks
to make a cross for the gravesite.

I said a prayer, *Lord, please*
watch over this small bird

and may its soul rest in peace.
When I looked over my son was crying.

I hugged him, said these things happen
and he said he knew, then ran

inside and played video games for an hour
while I made dinner. Now it's late,

and I've had two glasses of wine, and he's asking
how birds fly, so I say they have wings, muscles

like we have legs and muscles
that allow us to walk and he looks

at me and says *if we're like the birds
are you going to die?* and I say *some day*

but not today or anytime soon
and he says *it's like magic isn't it*

what's that, Trevor?
how birds can fly, he says

And I think muscle and bone and nerve synapse.
I think five years old, and I say *yes*

it is like magic, all of it, as I stand
to turn out the lights.

Midnight Stroll

She would wait until my father was asleep,
then pluck me from my bed, lead me around
the neighborhood, smelling of wine and cigarettes.
She would tell me about the people who lived
in the houses we passed, which ones were cheating
on their spouses, which ones came home for lunch every day.
She would tell me about my father too, how he had been
a great potter once but he'd given it up to pay the rent.
I didn't know if anything she said was true, or if that even mattered.
She was my mother, it was after midnight, I was seven years old,
and together we walked the dark night, hand in hand,
while all around us the world slept.

Walking into Work

As I walk into work today, the Medical
Examiner's van passes, carting off another
one that didn't make it. I work at a hospital,
so death itself should not surprise me.

Still, shouldn't it account for more?
Shouldn't we slow down for a moment
or two: silence, peace, a pause
in our otherwise rolling along days?

Perhaps, but if so, not here, not today
because some unseen bird is singing,
the daffodils are rising, and me, I'm walking
as fast as I can to get to work on time.

On the 3rd Floor at Moses Cone Memorial Hospital

Pushing the portable X-ray machine
on my way to do a Stat chest on a Mr. Wilson
in 3002, I spotted two old ladies standing
in the hall, leaning against their IV poles.
They both had to be in their 70s, decked out
in loose hospital gowns, red skid-proof socks
stuffed into white slippers from home.

They were laughing as if this was where
they wanted to spend a Tuesday afternoon.
One of the ladies had white hair and the other red.
I didn't realize the red hair was a wig
until the white-haired lady reached up to straighten it,
as if to say, come on, let's get ourselves together here.
And the lady with the wig blushed
as if to say aren't we beyond all that now
and the other lady shook her head
as if to say no, we never really are.

Juncos

It snowed for two days
and each hour we tossed
out a handful of bird seed
they came, so many birds,
against the white sheet of our
backyard. A junco, so small
and grey, hopped to the
back door, opened and closed
his beak. When I opened
the door, he didn't fly away
but stayed there as if to say thanks
and I said you're welcome.
Two days later the snow was
gone, the juncos too.
Foolish to miss a bird,
but there it is, I do.

Playing Pool

After my parent's divorce, my father kept a pool table
in the living room of the house he rented. One night,

I climbed out of bed, crept down the hall
and watched him in his baggy white Jockeys

sink ten, twenty, thirty balls with ease.
I wondered why my mother couldn't see this

how she could kick him out. I was only fourteen
young and dumb enough to believe possessing

a certain skill was enough to make people love you.

At the Playground

My four-year-old doesn't play
with other kids; he lives in his
imagination, throws his hands
in the air, fingers writing the sky
like tiny birds, and when the other
children turn and stare, I want
to tell him to stop doing that,
to just ride down the damn slide, swing
on the swings like everyone else,
but he is only being himself,
someone I'm still not comfortable with.

Sophomore Biology

dissecting frogs and what I wanted
was to see the inside of a thing
how its heart kept beating when
all around there was heartbreak,
Dina saying we should be friends now
Dad saying he was going to move out for a bit
and there lay the frog, flayed open, white,
no blood, but of course, this was
something without a beating heart
because those we don't get to see
and all we can do is imagine
the way they squeeze and beat and open
and close and there is Mr. Moore
at the front of the class
talking kidney, talking liver, lungs, all these organs
that meant nothing to me when all I ever wanted
was to get to the heart of things.

Turtles

We cheered on the baby sea turtles,
wished them safe passage
on their fifty-foot journey
from nest to sea, and you said we had to go,
you needed to talk to your mother,
needed to tell her what you'd seen
on that beach, and in the hotel
I heard you on the phone, crying,
saying you were ready to come home,
and I thought of the baby turtles,
the one I named Felix, the way
he pawed at the dirt, pushed it aside,
sure of his destination, and I hoped
he would make it even if we did not.

Each Night, After Work

my father would head out to his
shed for an hour or two. I never
knew what he did out there and when
I asked my mother she said *he works*
hard, needs a few minutes to himself.
But is he building a rocket ship out there?
She laughed, *no, but I think he would like to.*
But what does he do?
She repeated, *he needs a few minutes*
to himself; it's not easy being a father.

It's been at least forty years since that
conversation, but I'm thinking about it as
I sit in my car at the park two blocks
from the house I share with my wife and son.
I've started stopping here on the way home
from work, sitting under the oak trees,
watching the kids play basketball and soccer.
I hadn't meant to carry on this tradition,
only stopped one day to catch my breath
before pulling into my driveway.

Reason for Exam

When I asked her why
we were doing a chest X-ray
this morning, she said
Hell if I know, so I asked
why she was in the hospital.
My daughter thinks I'm sick,
she said. *But you feel all right?*
I asked and she looked at me,
coughed long enough to produce
a good chunk of phlegm,
spit it into the pink basin
and said *I'm right as rain,*
my boy, right as wet-ass rain.

More Lives

My son is playing Mario 64
when he starts to cry, says he needs
more lives, that he wants to beat
the game and save the princess.
I tell him it's all right, it's just a game
but he shakes his head, says I don't
understand.

What I want to tell him is this is only
the beginning. You'll spend your life
wanting more lives, different lives,
you'll want to be the quarterback dating
the cheerleader, you'll want to be a pilot
or a doctor, a baker, or even, God forbid,
a poet, but we only get one life
and this one, the real one, will probably be nothing
at all like he imagines.

But I don't tell him this.
He's only eight, a boy who
is young enough to believe
in videogames, to believe he is capable
of anything, even saving a princess
with his bare hands.

So It Begins

My mother and father
in the parking lot of Toby
Hospital, on a snow-swept
January Massachusetts morning
she cries, *it's time*, from
the backseat, but my father
only wants the warmth of this car,
the safety of this life before a new one,
says *let me finish this cigarette,*
just a minute, for Christsakes
but apparently I can't wait
because my mother cries out again
as I appear head-first
on the rough cloth seats
the windows cloudy with steam
my mother's warm tears,
lips up against my own.
Outside it's so cold, all you could see,
they tell me now, is a wall of white snow.

Help Desk

I'm working the IT help desk
when a nurse at the Woman's Hospital
calls and tells me her boyfriend
broke up with her, so I say
is your computer working?
Are you able to complete
your patient documentation?
She says *six months and he dumps me*
a week before Christmas.
But your computer, ma'am,
is it working okay? She says
but what I am going to tell my mother
she loved him more than she loves me.
What I should say is you've
called the wrong number
and gently hang up the phone,
but I don't. Instead, I ask
his name and she says *Ray*
and I lean back in my chair,
close my eyes and listen even though
I know I probably won't be able to help her.

Breakfast with My Mother the Morning After My Father Died

They'd been divorced five years
both already remarried with new lives
but still I could see the pain
on her face. The way she sipped
her coffee, smoked her cigarette.
She tried to start a sentence
say the things that needed saying.
I was seventeen, only wanted
to get back to my room and my guitar
pretend for a little while he wasn't
gone. *You look just like him,* she said.
I leaned over, took her hand in mine.
She squeezed. I squeezed back.
For a while this was enough.

Consultation Room

the chaplain does his best
to get the names of the mothers and fathers,
the brothers and sisters,
and he listens to their questions,
how does this happen to good college bound kids?
why were they out driving at two in the morning?
knows if he wanted to answer them
he could not. All he can offer are the
simple, tangible things of life: an ear,
some tissue, a shoulder, his two strong arms.

I'm True

my six-year-old says,
meaning I'm telling the truth.

I correct him in the way fathers
are supposed to: *You should
really say I'm telling the truth.*

But he shakes his head, folds
arms tight across his chest and says,
No Dad, I'm true, really, I'm true.

I start to correct him again, then
catch myself, say, *Yes, I know,
Trevor. You are true.*

Plums

My wife and I are throwing
plums at each other. They
are wild plums, no bigger than
a grape, from a tree in our backyard.
At first, it's for fun, but then
she hits me in the throat and it stings
so I throw harder, aim for her head
and when I hit her left ear
she cries out and I run toward her,
ashamed and afraid of what I've done,
but as I reach her she releases another
handful, hits me in the forehead, the eye,
and I fall to the ground, grab my eye,
hear her laugh as the back door
slams shut, leaving me on the ground
wounded and laughing, unable to see,
but already plotting my revenge.

Downy Woodpecker

Outside my kitchen window
the downy woodpecker settles
in, works his way through the
peanut butter suet, looks up at
me once, as if deciding whether or not
he needs to fly away. Thankfully,
he stays, eats it all, as I'd hoped he would.

Amnesia

He breathes into the desk,
leans over the white page
sharpened pencil in hand
mug of Earl Grey cooling
beside him but back to the paper,
which is blank except for one word
in the upper right corner
Draw, so he begins
moves his hand up and down.
Lines and shapes begin to form.
The bending of his wrist,
the familiar motion—
on the page a cow appears
then a tree, a boy, and over
to the right there's a horse
head bent to the grass.
But let's get back
to the barefooted boy,
ten or eleven, walking
toward the horse with
a handful of wet carrots
suspended in time like
the artist himself. He'd
like to know if the boy is him
but he's long given up thoughts
of knowing, remembering.
It doesn't matter anyway
The lines are drawn.
The boy is reaching.
The horse still looking at the grass
and the sun, if you could see
it, so bright and radiant above
the whole lot of this
small and perfect world.

Thankful

My wife finds the milkweed leaves dotted
with tiny white butterfly eggs and brings them inside,
transfers the milkweed to an aquarium to protect
the eggs from birds. In a day or two the caterpillars hatch,
and when they're ready to form their chrysalis
she lines the top of the aquarium with
Maxi-pads so they can spin their thin life line
hang for thirteen days and then we
watch them emerge as butterflies.

She lets me release one and my throat catches
as the monarch lights on my finger, its flimsy wings
flapping in the air before it lifts up and out
into the backyard. I am thankful my wife
takes the time to look for white dots on the back
of milkweed leaves, how she let me witness
this transformation, thankful for the
feather-light butterfly on my finger
before it heads out into the world.

Work

When my son asks about my day,
I say it was fine but think about
the man I X-rayed whose arm got
caught in a machine at the Merita
Bread factory. The skin on his
forearm was peeled back from wrist
to elbow, both radius and ulna fractured.
My son is only nine and doesn't
yet need to know how you can head off
to work one day and return home
hours later, your life changed forever.
He'll learn all that soon enough.

2

Crabapple Trees

I stand among the row of crabapple trees
in bloom on the west side of the hospital

and the tree's pink, red and white petals
float through the air, brushing my face

I breathe them in, steadying myself
for six more hours in the pediatric unit

for those kids who keep trying
even after their bodies have given up.

Later when they are asleep
and their parents gone home for a quick

shower or down to the cafeteria
I lift a few of the petals from my scrub pockets

sprinkle them over Malcolm and Kate and Luke
like fairy dust, like hope, something

I'll take in any form I can get.

Fish Father

My father is a fish
below the surface
in murky water.
He rises occasionally
to eat, to splash
in the cool wash of our
family. My father, like
a satisfied bass, will
rarely strike the bait
you offer. He's more
likely to play with your
worms, minnows. He has
his own food down there.

Cicadas on the Sidewalk, Late August

They line the sidewalks
belly up or prone
propped up on
their tiny black feet
wings chewed off,
bodies bit in half
as if bird food, ant food
hard to believe
only two weeks ago
they were so strong
as they sang their
deafening summer song.

When They Tell Me

I know it's true,
have always known
his lack of caring for others,
the spinning and hands flying,
the stemming and figure eights
so when they tell me,
all those people gathered
in a room, I'm not surprised
because I'd known it all along
but had hoped I was wrong.

Peaches

are what she wanted in the end
said they reminded her of South
Carolina that summer she was
fifteen, living with her Auntie
Josephine in a white clapboard
house at the end of a dirt road.
They'd pick cotton during the day,
eat peaches for lunch, her fingers
sticky the rest of the afternoon.
There was a boy who worked the farm,
Jerri, who kissed her one July afternoon
and then never returned to work.
There were thunderstorms, she said
so quick and fierce, all you could do
was lay in the fields and let the rain
wash your dirty face, your hair,
pray you didn't get struck by lightning.
And dogs would appear, follow behind
you for an hour or two then disappear.
Her aunt would walk out into the field
with a wicker basket of peaches, smiling,
saying take two, take three and she took
all she could stomach. In this nursing
home, now, I don't have anything to give her
except my time, my ears for her stories,
so on my next visit I bring her a peach
and she lifts it to her nose, smells the sweetness
beneath the surface, rubs it against her cheek,
a scene so private I have to look away.

My Father's Golf Clubs

My father's golf clubs are tucked away
in my attic, beside the old paint cans
and beach chairs and suitcases.
He used these clubs on the day he died
playing golf, almost twenty years ago now.
After his death, my stepmother gave the clubs
to my uncle, who years later gave them to me.
And then when my wife and I moved into our home
a decade ago, I set them in a corner of the attic.

A couple times a year, always while searching
for something else, I will spot those clubs.
May even pull out his rust-specked putter
or the 7-Wood with the cracked rubber grip,
squeeze it in my hands and imagine him playing
his final round. I wonder if he played well that day,
if he was under or over par.

Femur Fracture on a 3-Month-Old

They say the baby wouldn't stop
crying and Mom noticed his right leg
was swollen this morning as she changed
his diaper. He lies still as a stuffed animal
while I hold him down for the X-ray.

As Rachel makes the exposure, I look over at Mom,
at Dad, but they aren't looking at each other.
And while I would like to blame the father—
it's usually the father, isn't it?—this time I don't know.
There's something about this girl and her Iron Maiden t-shirt
and arms folded tight across her chest that rubs me wrong.

It will come out, what really happened. It always does
because by the time we get back to the Peds ER,
their room will be filled with Police and social workers
and one of these parents will crack.

But for a moment I forget all that, cast it far
into the future, as I bend over to remove
the tiny lead shield from the baby's pelvis
and he looks me in the eye. How bright
and alive his eyes are as they search my face
for something—help or hope or answers to questions
he can't yet begin to understand—and I keep
staring down at him, until I feel Mom step up
and take her baby into her skinny little arms,
reminding me my bit part in this drama is over.

I Loved the Apartment on Elm

Because you were there
And we had a cat named Scout
A window that opened
To the back of the Dunkin' Donuts factory
Where the stench of sweetness
Rose up, into our apartment
Close the window, you'd say
I can't even breathe in here
And then you were gone
Scout died years later
They moved the factory
across town to a cheaper location.

But I miss Scout; and I miss you
And I miss the donut factory workers
Groups of two and three who would
Come outside to smoke on breaks
Men and women, white, black, Hispanic
In white smocks, hairnets, beard nets
The way they would laugh
Or cough or cry or cuss
Huddled in a circle against all that
Sweetness. Once, this old guy spotted
me watching. He flipped me the bird
Told me to go fuck myself
Hell, I even miss him.

Ice Cream Truck

At the ice cream truck
my son surveys the selections
decides on a raspberry snow cone
when I ask for a lick,
a small taste,
he looks over at me,
pauses,
as if considering whether or not
to deny me this small favor
and while he doesn't today
I know it won't be long before he does.

What She Could See

When she was little,
she would climb the oak tree
in her backyard, sit tight against the branches
and watch the world of her family.
She'd watch her sister kiss boys
on the back porch, watch their hands
disappear into her sister's shirt and shorts,
the way she'd grab their forearms
as if she wanted them to stop,
and the girl watched her father practice
his golf swing in the backyard,
the way he'd bring his gloved hand
to his eyes as if watching an imaginary ball
coast off into the distance,
and she watched her mother
sit on the porch, smoking a cigarette
and whispering into her cell phone,
the way she would laugh, then look
around, as if happiness was something
she needed to hide.

Out Back, Behind the Hospital

We shared cigarettes and jokes
talked about anything except
what we'd seen, the baby we'd X-rayed,
his bruises, his broken arm,
the way he'd opened his mouth to cry
but no sound came, his tears, his eyes wide
but still he didn't make a sound.
At 2 months old, he'd already learned
the importance of silence, so out back
behind the hospital, Fred and I talked
about the Super Bowl, where we'd
like to go skiing, our plans for the weekend,
anything but what we'd seen yet had no words for.

Penguin Pigeon

Driving beneath the bridge
I spotted a grey bird and said *penguin*.
My wife laughed and said *pigeon*,
repeating it, *pigeon*, as if speaking to an idiot.
She sighed and turned to the window,
staring at something I could not see.

I considered saying it was a mistake,
a simple slip of the tongue, of course
I knew the difference between a penguin
and pigeon, but the time for stating my case
seemed to have already passed.

In the NICU

The baby was brain dead
but they wanted a chest X-ray to check
his lungs for organ donation.
His hands were no bigger than a plum
and his chest seemed almost translucent,
barely hiding the still-beating organs.
As the nurse lifted him for me to slide
the X-ray cassette under we looked at each
other, our faces no more than six inches apart
her red hair pulled behind her right ear.
The two of us as close, as intimate, as lovers,
sharing the stale air over his lifeless body.
Her eyes were full of tears, and while
I didn't cry then, later, back in Radiology
in the thin shielding light of the darkroom,
waiting for the X-ray film to process,
I cried harder than I ever had before
and when I was done I wiped my eyes,
my face, before walking back
out into the bright light
and all that was waiting for me.

The Zoo

On a trip to the North Carolina Zoo
my son asks me why the baboon's
butt is so red and I tell him I don't know.
He asks me why they keep the roadrunner
in a glass dome and I say *Because it's a zoo,*
so he asks me to help the bird escape
and when I tell him I can't, *The bird wouldn't even*
know how to live in our part of the world,
he looks at me with something close to hate
says he's ready to go, he's seen more
than enough for one day, that he thought
I was someone else, someone who cared.

Secrets

Come and tell me your secrets
she says, *tell me what*
you are most ashamed of,
so I tell her about you,
your long black hair, your
blue sheets lifted over our heads
brown socks and purple underwear
I tell her about apple butter and walnut bread
and your apartment, that place I escaped
to all those months ago, about how you brought
me back to life and then later I refused your calls
about the day you appeared at my home
and I pretended I didn't even know you.

The First Patient I Saw Die

was this bone-skinny guy
mid-fifties, dark hair
wet with sweat and
when I arrived in ICU
with my portable X-ray machine
his room was crowded
with doctors and nurses
as he looked around, wide-eyed,
his O2 mask whistling
while Ryan, the Lead Resident,
squeezed his right hand,
told him to relax,
said he was going to be alright.
When the man scanned
the room his eyes landed on me
and though I wanted to
I couldn't hold his stare
so I turned away
and when the alarms started,
I got the hell out of there.

The Wren in May

The wren is tiny and brown and perfect
perched on the bush outside my bay
window, he calls and calls, then drops
from sight for a minute, returns wet, shakes
it off and when he repeats this I realize he is
taking a bath in my cat's shallow water bowl
and again he is there, up on the branch,
three feet from me, his curved beak,
wet feathers, and for a few moments
I love this bird more than I love anything
else in the world. He reminds me of someone,
some time and it's only later in bed with my
wife asleep beside me, that I do remember—
a Thursday, thirty years ago, my ten-year-old
son is stepping out of the shower
his hair pointing this way and that,
eyelids dripping, his face perfect and
smiling as he accepts the towel I offer him.

What a Photo Tells Us

I recently found a photo of myself sitting
on a pony. It's from my 7th birthday,
and in the background I can see the house I grew up in.

This is the house where my parents fought,
where I stood outside my sister's window
one summer afternoon and listened to her
have sex with a skinny boy who wore glasses.

I can see the old AC unit, hanging
out of our living room window, the one I ran into
and ended up in the ER with thirteen stitches.

I can see the three palm trees along the side
of the house. They were knocked over during Hurricane
Andrew and the last one there landed on top
of my father's old yellow VW bug.

I can see the Byrds' house, next door, where I'd gone
to play spin the bottle, hoping for a chance
to kiss Donna but instead it was her brother, George,
who held me down and pressed his lips against mine.

And I can see the driveway where my father
drove away from us for good that night after a dinner
of ham steak and corn and mashed potatoes.

While I can see all that in this photo, and remember
it clearly, I cannot recall this birthday, the feeling
of sitting on a pony, of that cowboy outfit, the friends that
must have come that day, if not for me then for the chance
to see a pony in our boring old neighborhood.

Junior

To be named after your father
is supposed to be an honor,
and it can feel like it
when you follow him into the bar
and the other men pat him, and you,
on the back, say *about damn time you got here, Steve.*
But what about when you're at his funeral
and the preacher says your name over and over
as he talks about your dead father,
and you can't help but feel like it is you,
or a piece of you, they are lowering
into the ground forever?

Peach Fuzz

Not quite a mustache
a thin line of facial hair
above my son's upper lip.
I catch him this morning
looking in the mirror,
running his finger
across the line of peach fuzz
what you got there? I ask
and he says *nothing*.
is that a mustache?
and he says *no*.
An hour later,
over breakfast,
he looks up
from his pancakes and bacon, asks,
does it look like a mustache?
a little, I say, and he doesn't
say anything else, lowers his
head back to his plate
but still I see the smile
he's trying to hide.

In Training

It was my first job as an X-ray tech and
Miguel told me to always look busy,
to carry an X-ray cassette and lift
it in the air when I walked by the supervisor.
He said to keep moving, never stop
long enough for them to give you more work.

Miguel was forty years older than me,
riding out his last few years before retirement
while I was just a kid, trying to learn
how to work and live and for reasons
I still can't understand they put me
with him, a man with a strong heart
and tired, old legs that never stopped moving.

Grandfather

And later, I visited him
at the trailer park he owned
in Pinellas Park, Florida, and together
we travelled by golf cart down
Stevie Lane and *Kimberly Court,*
roads he'd named after my sister and me,
and we passed a pony and an alligator
passed other golf carts, three-wheeled bicycles
propelled forward by neighbors
whose names he'd forgotten,
and when we reached the end,
there in his covered driveway
he asked me to go inside for some water.
When I returned, he was slumped
over the steering wheel
his forehead pressed against
his white driving gloves
and before I said a word, before I woke him,
I thought of the man he used to be
back when he was still the King of Wareham
and we drove the streets of that Massachusetts town
in his baby blue convertible Cadillac
back when I was his sidekick, his grandson,
the likely heir to his trailer park dynasty.

Playing Catch

When my son says
he doesn't like sports
I say, *I know, I know*
but you should learn
how to throw a baseball
and he gives me a look
that says *but why,*
this is stupid, Dad.
Still he follows me outside
and we toss the ball
back and forth. The spring
day is as fine as you can
imagine, cool and blue skied,
chickadees flying past us
to feed their young
my knees don't ache
my heart for a little while beats
with a familiar perfect rhythm
until my wife says *what*
are you doing, and I blink.
I'm standing in my back yard,
alone, throwing this old
baseball up in the air
and catching it, squeezing
my glove tight, holding
on to this moment as long as I can.

Owls

For the third night in a row we gather
at my neighbor's to watch the owls roost.
There are six of us. We stretch out in
our lawn chairs, drink beer or wine
and look up at the hole in the tall oak
and wait for the male to arrive. When he does,
we sigh as he starts his low and steady *whoo, whoo,*
calling for her. We watch, we wait, and when she
does not come we slowly, one by one, stand
and walk back to our houses. An hour later,
I look outside and see my neighbor—an avid birdwatcher
and recent widow—still standing in her backyard.
I walk over and say *Barbara,* and she shakes her head
and begins to cry, so I hug her, and she says
How could she and I say *It's just the way things are*
and she says *You don't know what the hell you're talking about*
and I think she's right as I hold her, waiting,
willing that damn bird to get here and show her face.

3

In The Hospital Cafeteria

We lived on fried chicken
drippy macaroni and cheese,
egg salad sandwiches
on white Wonder bread
none of it a joy to look at or eat
but we weren't there for fine dining
we were searching for sustenance
something to buoy us
against the demands of the day
the patients who never stopped coming
the gap between what we needed to know
and what we did know and
through it all there was Charles
serving lunch and William dinner
both guys from the local group home
in their starched white chef outfits
hats tilted left or right
depending on the day
and we gladly took what they gave us
happy for some small solace
their familiar head nod or wink
the brown food trays
the grey garbage cans marked trash
the blues ones labeled recycle
in this place we were trying to make our own.

In Our Third Year of Marriage

When I ask if you'd like another glass of wine
you look at me longer than necessary
say no, you think we've both had enough
and I say *okay*, pour myself another anyway
walk into the other room, back to this novel I've
been reading while you go back to Netflix,
to your laptop, to whatever it is you do without me.

Hospital Hopscotch

No one knows where it came from,
a hopscotch board on a sidewalk,
leading into the children's hospital,
but as quick as it appeared, so did
the children, laughing and hopping,
in their hospital gowns and isolation masks,
holding onto their IV poles for balance
as they count the boxes and hop, hop
all the way from one to ten and back again.

Blanket Bubble

My son's favorite
thing to do is hide
under his Mario blanket
and play videogames.
All you can see
is this lump in the sheets,
a knee moving here,
his head bobbing there,
and when I try to
squeeze in with him
he says *No, Dad, there's
not enough room for you*
and while this is true
still it surprises and hurts me
more than it should.

What My Dead Father and I Would Talk About

The weather, the Tampa Bay Rays
and we would drink a beer,
or perhaps many beers,
Busch Light, of course,
and find a boxing match on ESPN
we watched a lot of Marvin Hagler
fights back in the 80s, and we'd
stay up late for a West Coast ball game
maybe the Dodgers-Giants
or Dodgers-Padres.
I'd fall asleep first
because I never could
keep up with my old man.
Wake with a crick in my neck,
wonder if it had all been a dream,
the dozen empty beer cans on the table,
the smell of bacon frying in the kitchen.
My father standing bare-chested
in his Jockeys at the stove.

I Don't Know

I don't know how to tie
the knots my son needs
for his merit badge,
don't know how to start a campfire
or properly build a fort or tree house,
to stand tall and strong against the wind,
but I know how to hold him close
feel the heat and weight of his body
against mine.
Perhaps that's enough.
Some say no.
I say yes.

Another Father Poem

The year before he died
my father owned a bar
I'd watch him talk to
the beer reps
the drunk customers
the pool players
and dart throwers.
But when he came home
he stopped talking
as if he'd said all he could
in that dark, dinghy place
He was happy that year
and then he lost the bar
a few months later we lost him too
as if he'd done all he needed to do.

Dream Job

Last week a baby was brought
in with 29 cigarette burns,
each no bigger than a pencil
eraser, all over his body.

When I asked the mother
about the burns, she said
We do it when he's bad
or won't stop crying.

This doesn't surprise me
because I've seen it so many times
and she looks like all the other
mothers who have told me such things,
strung-out and nail-biting nervous.

But what I'll never understand
is why she cries, and even
seems surprised, when
we take her baby away.

Morning Light

In the dark morning kitchen
pouring myself a cup of coffee
I hear her voice, the quiet tired *hello*.
I turn to the table and at first
all I see is a shape, but eventually
she comes in to focus, elbows
on the table, tea mug against
her right cheek, the glow
of the streetlight above her head.

How could I have walked by
and not seen this woman whom
I've spent more than half my life with?
I tell myself it's the darkness,
the lack of sleep and caffeine,
but even I don't believe that.

Another Hospital Poem

Tonight, at the hospital,
the patients are laughing,
none of their IV's are occluded,
they say please and thank you
and can all go to the bathroom by themselves.

Mr. Hughes in 3010
is no longer dying. He's sitting up
in bed, ventless and free, playing
bridge with his wife and son, Pete,
who died decades ago in Vietnam.

Your frequent flyer,
Diabetic-Larry
fell asleep early,
so he can't say,
my, my, nurse Jane,
please come over here
I've got an itch that needs scratching
can't brush his thick fingers
against your thin scrubs

But forget about Mr. Hughes and Larry
because Mrs. Seneca in 3002
has stopped asking for cigarettes
and is offering you a red tulip
she picked in the hospital's garden.
When you lift the flower
to your nose, you close your eyes
hold them tight as long as you can
because you know what you'll find
once you open them again.

Silent Time

Eating lunch with my son
in the elementary school cafeteria
I am struck by the volume of children.
Their willingness to talk louder and louder,
over one another. My son is telling me about
his spelling test, about how he thinks he did pretty well.

But then the piano starts, indicating silent time,
a five-minute reprieve from the noise and chatter
of children's voices, their lives and concerns
as important to them as their parents' own worries.
For a few minutes they go back to their peanut butter
and jelly sandwiches, their crackers and cheese sticks,
100-calorie snack packs of cookies and chips.

They seem to know when silent time is coming to an end
because from nowhere I hear the first low rumble
and then the piano has stopped and the chorus
of a hundred young voices calls out, and this time
it sounds as beautiful as anything I've ever heard.

Spring

She'd like an apple this morning
perhaps not first thing—there is coffee
and toast and maybe even a hard-boiled egg
but after her breakfast and walking the dog
and getting the kids ready for school
she'd like to come home and sit on the white
wicker chair beside the window and eat a Fuji apple,
watch the birds at the feeder, her cat chasing
the catkins, floating, flying through the light April air.

Red Wine

We spent the winter sampling red wines,
some we liked but most we didn't.
Neither of us had ever been wine drinkers
I preferred beer; margaritas were your thing
but we'd read the reports about the health
benefits of red wine and both approaching
fifty decided it was time to try. Each night
we'd drink a glass and sometimes two
discuss the flavors as if we knew what
we were talking about: *too dry, too sweet,
too bubbly*, both of us wondering what we were
doing, both of us happy, after twenty-seven
years of marriage, to try something new.

Grace

The old couple shuffled into the hospital cafeteria.
He was pale and thin with a bandage on his right forearm,
a yellow patient ID bracelet on his wrist.
He stood beside her at the counter while she
scooped them each a cup of broccoli soup
and poured glasses of sweet tea. At the cashier he reached
for his wallet, but she pushed his hand aside as if to say
let me take care of this, but when he reached in his pocket again,
she let him, knowing how important it was for him
to do this in a cafeteria they hoped never to visit again.

Biopsy

When the dermatologist tells you
the biopsy came back benign
you stop listening to what else
he has to say, to his warnings, his recommendations,
because you are already on your boat
in Mosquito Lagoon, a cool Bud in one hand,
your fishing pole in the other,
the sun on your naked back,
and there's a huge redfish on your line
and you're fighting it, not about
to give up, holding on for dear life.

Hawk

Driving to work, I spotted
the red-tailed hawk perched on the stop sign

at the corner of Courtland & Adams.
Surveying the suburban yards

for his next meal, he looked in my direction,
then turned away, disinterested.

I lowered my eyes to check the time
and when I looked up again he was gone,

leaving me alone in the warm comfort of my car,
delighted by what I'd seen,

desperate for his return.

My Wife Plants Trees for the Dead

There's the saucer magnolia for her father
the cherry tree for her grandmother
and another one for our neighbor Linda
A camellia for her Aunt Glennis.
In the back corner is a pin oak for my father,
a man she never met. I ask her what
she'll plant for me when I die and she says
probably a tulip or something small.
But that's not a tree, I say, *is it because*
I'm special to you and she laughs
says, *no, it's so I won't have to look at you*
all year long. I'd like to think she was joking.

The Truth About Birds and Marriage

On my friend's wedding day,
a pair of waxwings flew into his bay window.
We were at his house, on the side of the mountain,
listening to the preacher explain the importance
of marriage and vows when we heard the thud and turned.
The bride's mother was a vet and she said
to put the birds in a brown paper bag.
She said they were probably only stunned and needed
the darkness and quiet to recover. And eventually,
as we drank and danced, there was a rustling in the bag,
so we opened it and the birds flew up and away and we cheered.

Years later, when my friend and his wife
were in the middle of a divorce a few of our friends
said those birds were a bad omen. But I've been married
long enough now to know it wasn't a pair of birds
crashing into the window that doomed them.
It's usually nothing as dramatic as that
but more the slow winding down of a marriage,
the way it can be chipped away at day after day
and whether or not it's going to last has about as much to do
with birds crashing into windows as it does plain dumb luck.

My Mother's Bologna Sandwich

I can still see her standing at the stove
a cigarette between her thin lips, a spatula
ready to flip the sandwich, the room filling with steam
and smoke, the cheese on top,
another slice of buttered Wonder bread
and like magic the sandwich is in front of me
cut at an angle. *Here Mom*, I say, *have
a bite* and she lifts her hand, her cigarette,
as if that was all she ever needed. But I insist
and her bite is small and mouse-like when all
I ever wanted was to give her the whole damn thing.

Red-Bellied Sapsucker

My wife calls me to the bay window
to see the red-bellied sapsucker
says, *look, look,* as if I don't know
what she's referring to, how our son
used to run around the house
yelling *sapsucker, sapsucker,*
a word she'd taught him
a word he loved to catch and
release from his small mouth.
I can't recall the last time I'd seen
a sapsucker, or heard him call
for one, but when my wife says
sapsucker I say it too, close my eyes,
hear our boy filling the quiet
rooms of our house once again.

Boring

After X-raying the dying boy, I called home
and spoke to my seven-year-old son,
a boy taller and funnier
than I would have ever imagined.

He told me he was bored, there was nothing
on TV and too much homework to do.
I wanted to tell him to forget about homework,
and that damn TV, to go outside and smell the air,
roll around in the grass, but I didn't.

Instead, I drove home on my dinner break
and helped him with his math homework.
The chance to hold him, to smell his hair,
feel his weight against me.

I kissed him on the forehead, then drove
blurry-eyed back to the hospital
where nothing is ever as boring
or perfect as what we leave behind.

Acknowledgements

I would like to thank the editors of the publications in which these poems, some in slightly different forms, first appeared:

American Journal of Nursing: "The First Patient I Saw Die"
Aries: "Silent Time," and "More Lives"
Bellevue Literary Review: "Out Back, Behind the Hospital"
Blood & Thunder: "On The 3rd Floor at Moses Cone Memorial Hospital"
Broad River Review: "Owls"
Chest: "Femur Fracture on a 3-Month-Old" and "Walking Into Work"
Eno: "Juncos," "Downy Woodpecker," and "Wrenn In May"
Flagler Review: "My Wife Plants Trees for the Dead"
Flash UK: "Penguin Pigeon"
Harmony Magazine: "Grace" "Biopsy," "Hospital Hopscotch," "Dream Job," and "Work"
The Healing Muse: "In the Hospital Cafeteria"
Iodine Poetry Journal: "Help Desk," "Plums," and "My Mother's Bologna Sandwich"
Journal of Medical Humanities: "In the NICU" and "Another Hospital Poem"
Kakalak: "Crabapple Trees," "What She Sees," and "Secrets"
Main Street Rag: "Grandfather" and "Boring"
O. Henry: "At the Playground," "How Do Birds Fly," "Hawk," and "Sophomore Biology"
The Olive Press: "Amnesia" and "So It Begins"
One Hundred Word Story: "Morning Light"

Pinesong: "Consultation Room" and "Thankful"

Pinestraw: "My Father's Golf Clubs"

Poetry in Plain Sight: "Ice Cream Truck" and "Turtles"

Prelude: "What My Dead Father and I Would Talk About"

Prose Poem: "Midnight Stroll" and "Junior"

Salt: "The Truth About Birds and Marriage"

Snapdragon: "Cicadas on the Sidewalk, Late August"

Stoneboat Journal: "What a Photo Tells Us"

Taking Flight: "Spring"

The Waiting Room Reader: "I'm True"

The Way To My Heart: "Red Wine"

Tishman Review: "Red-Bellied Sapsucker"

Biographical Sketch

Steve Cushman earned his MA from Hollins University and MFA from UNC-Greensboro. He has published four works of fiction, including the 2004 Novello Literary Award winning novel, *Portisville*, and most recently the novel, *Hopscotch*. His first full-length poetry collection, *How Birds Fly*, is the winner of the 2018 Lena Shull Book Award. After working as an X-ray Technologist for twenty years, he currently works in the IT Department at Moses Cone Memorial Hospital. Cushman lives in Greensboro, North Carolina, with his family.

The Lena M. Shull Book Contest

The Lena M. Shull Book Contest, sponsored by the North Carolina Poetry Society, is an annual contest for a full-length poetry manuscript written by a resident of North Carolina. The manuscript must not have been previously published, although individual poems within the collection may have been published elsewhere.

Made in the USA
Columbia, SC
15 August 2022

65363026R00059